GUINEA PIGS

Flora Gandolfo

Grolier
an imprint of

www.scholastic.com/librarypublishing

Published 2009 by Grolier
An Imprint of Scholastic Library Publishing
Old Sherman Turnpike,
Danbury, Connecticut 06816

For The Brown Reference Group plc
Project Editor: Jolyon Goddard
Editor: Katie John
Picture Researchers: Clare Newman, Sophie
Mortimer
Designer: Sarah Williams
Managing Editor: Tim Harris

Volume ISBN-13: 978-0-7172-8044-5
Volume ISBN-10: 0-7172-8044-6

**Library of Congress
Cataloging-in-Publication Data**

Nature's children. Set 5.
     p. cm.
  Includes index.
  ISBN-13: 978-0-7172-8084-1
  ISBN-10: 0-7172-8084-5 (set)
  1. Animals--Encyclopedias, Juvenile. 1.
Grolier Educational (Firm)
  QL49.N386 2009
  590.3--dc22

                           2008014674

Printed and bound in China

Contents

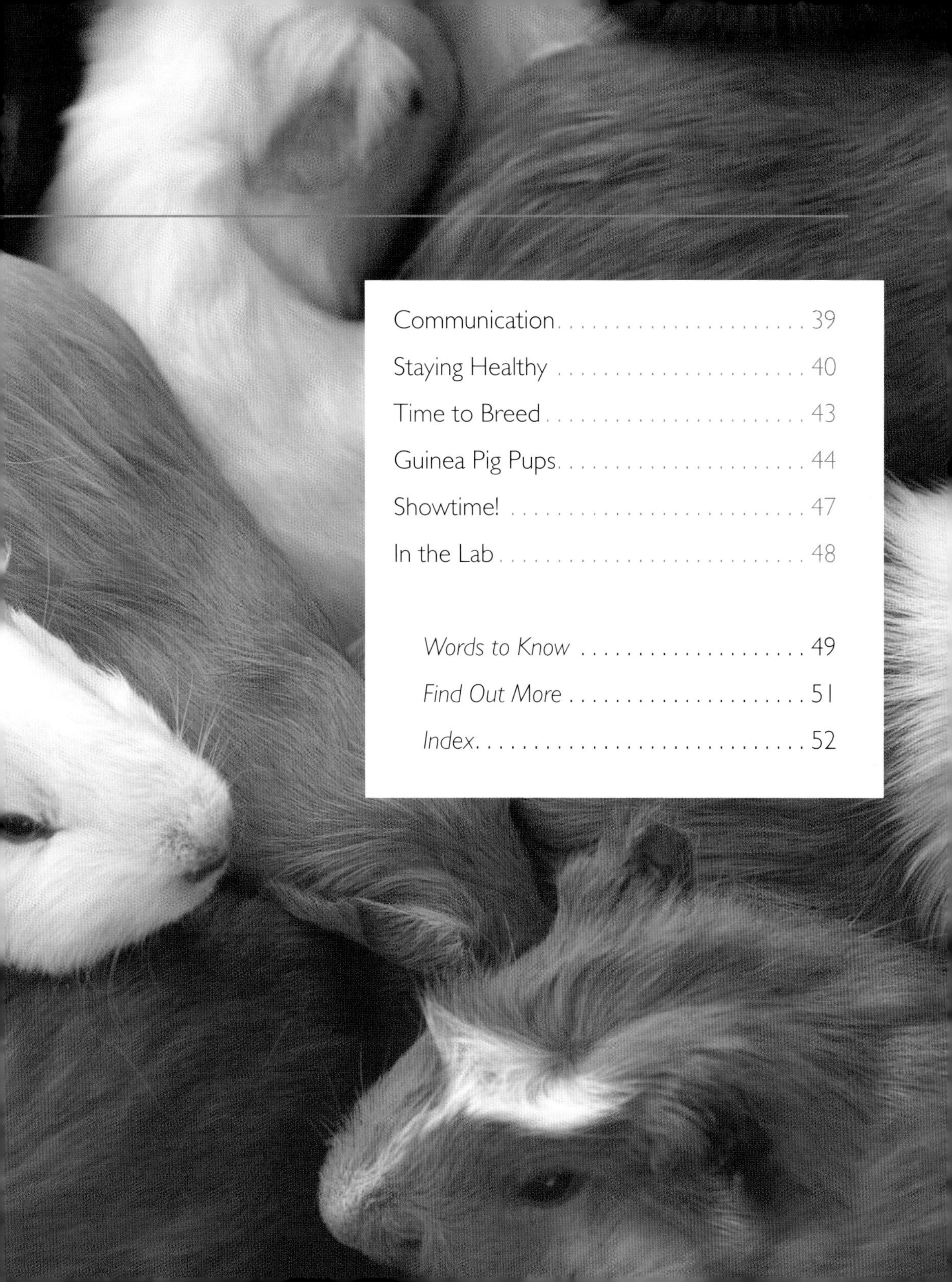

FACT FILE: Guinea Pigs

Class	Mammals (Mammalia)
Order	Rodents (Rodentia)
Family	Cavies (Caviidae)
Genus	Cavies and guinea pigs (*Cavia*)
Species	Domestic guinea pig (*Cavia porcellus*)
World distribution	Guinea pigs are kept as pets worldwide; in the wild, they live in South America
Habitat	Domestic guinea pigs are kept in cages; in the wild, guinea pigs live in grasslands, marshlands, and rocky regions
Distinctive physical characteristics	Compact, rounded body; short legs; small ears; eyes on sides of head; no visible tail
Habits	Shy animals; continually gnawing bark and other wood; communicate with one another by squeals and grunts
Diet	Pet guinea pigs eat hay, fruits, vegetables, and special food pellets; wild cavies eat grasses, seeds, flowers, and fruits

Introduction

For hundreds of years, guinea pigs have played a part in people's lives. People in ancient civilizations even believed they had magical powers! Today, scientists use guinea pigs for medical research.

Guinea pigs are gentle, lively creatures that enjoy the company of humans and respond well to plenty of attention. With soft fur and beady brown eyes, they are cute to look at and very cuddly. All their great qualities make them very popular pets today.

Guinea pigs are sociable and enjoy company.

Guinea pigs are not related to pigs, but they have a few piglike features, such as a plump body and droopy ears.

What's in a Name?

Guinea pigs are not related to pigs. They are members of the rodent family, like mice and hamsters. Their scientific name is *Cavia porcellus*. *Porcellus* is Latin for "little pig." They are also known as **cavies**. Guinea pigs are originally from Peru, in South America.

Why are they called guinea pigs? For one thing, their squeals and grunts are sometimes compared to the sounds pigs make. Some people believe they are built a little like a miniature pig, with a chubby body, rounded back, short neck, and a very little tail. Also like pigs, male guinea pigs are known as **boars** and females as **sows**.

Nobody is sure where the term "guinea" comes from. One possible explanation is that it is a mispronunciation of the South American country Guyana.

Where's Home?

Today, there are many different varieties of
domestic, or pet, guinea pigs. All guinea pigs are
descendants of native South American cavies.
These animals still live wild today in grasslands
called pampas (PAM-PUSS), swamplands, forest
edges, and rocky areas.

People in the mountains of Peru started
to domesticate wild cavies about 7,000 years
ago. Guinea pigs were first brought to North
America and Europe 400 years ago by explorers
returning from expeditions to South America.
They became fashionable as exotic pets among
wealthy people. Today, they are popular as pets
all throughout the world.

A wild cavy in one of its natural habitats—the pampas of South America.

Guinea pigs need hard objects such as bits of wood to gnaw, to keep their incisors at the right length. If these teeth get too long, the guinea pig will be unable to eat.

10

Body Basics

Guinea pigs are small, stocky animals. Boars can weigh 1½ to 2½ pounds (0.7 to 1.2 kg) and grow to 8 to 10 inches (20 to 25 cm) long. Sows are usually slightly smaller, but look so similar that it can be very hard to tell males and females apart.

An adult guinea pig has 20 permanent teeth. Like all rodents, they have long **incisors** at the front of the mouth. Rodents' teeth grow continually, so the animals need to gnaw things to wear them down and keep them a comfortable length. In the wild, cavies chew on tree bark. It is important to give guinea pigs something to gnaw, like a piece of wood.

Guinea pigs' small paws have four **digits**, or toes, on the front feet and three on the hind feet. The toes have sharp claws. In the wild, the claws are worn down as the guinea pig runs around on rough surfaces. Pet guinea pigs, however, might need to have their claws trimmed.

Silky Locks

Guinea pigs' coats, or **pelts**, can come in an array of colors, lengths, and textures depending on the breed. Wild cavies are a gray-brown color called **agouti** (A-GOO-TI). Many domestic guinea pigs are this color, too. Pet guinea pigs also come in various other colors, such as black, white, cream, brown, red, and lilac and often in combinations of these. Coats that are one solid color are called **self**. **Nonself** coats have fur of two or three different colors.

Guinea pigs' coats are made up of at least five different types of hairs. Each type of hair has a different thickness and texture—from a fine, fluffy **undercoat** to a top coat of longer, coarse **guard hairs**. Some varieties of guinea pigs have short fur, while others have long, silky pelts.

Most guinea pigs don't mind being gently groomed, or brushed. Brushing helps keep their fur in good condition. Short-haired breeds are easier to care for because they need less grooming.

In long-haired guinea pigs, such as this Coronet, extra-long guard hairs cover the animal's body.

A small brush with fairly soft natural bristles is ideal for grooming guinea pigs.

Many Varieties

There are many varieties, or breeds, of pet guinea pigs. These breeds are defined by the kind of coat they have—short, long, or curly.

The most common short-haired breed is the American, also known as the English shorthair. This guinea pig has smooth, glossy fur. Another is the Abyssinian (A-BUH-SI-NEE-UN), which has a slightly longer coat, with swirls called **rosettes** in its fur.

Long-haired varieties include breeds like the Peruvian and the Silkie. Their straight, silky fur can grow up to 1 inch (1.2 cm) a month. It needs regular grooming to stop it from getting matted. Some owners like to carefully trim the hair if it grows too long, so it will not pick up dirt.

There are also curly haired varieties, and one of the most well-known breeds is the Texel.

Some breeds are raised especially for shows. These breeds need a lot of care and attention. Owners of show guinea pigs usually spend a lot of time grooming and caring for them.

Buying a Pet

Before you take home a pet guinea pig, the first thing you need to decide is whether you have enough time to give it the care it needs. Any pet requires commitment for the whole of its life. For guinea pigs, that means four to seven years—maybe even longer.

There are several options to choose from when looking for guinea pigs. A good place to buy them is from a breeder. Breeders make sure their animals are fit and healthy. They regularly handle the young ones from an early age so they are easier to keep as pets. Guinea pigs are also widely available in pet shops. It is best to buy guinea pigs that are just a few months old. At that age, they will be independent of their mother but young enough to adapt to your home.

Many rescue centers have guinea pigs that need a new home. A rescued animal might be especially shy and nervous. It will need extra-gentle care and plenty of attention to make it feel safe.

A young guinea pig stays near its mother. Good breeders will get young ones used to human contact from an early age.

A group of agouti cavies comes out at night. Cavies are happiest when they have others to play with.

Friends for Life

Although they are shy creatures, guinea pigs are very sociable. In nature, wild cavies live in small groups called herds, usually with several sows and a boar. At home, it is a good idea to have at least two guinea pigs living in the same pen, so they will not get lonely.

Usually, groups of two or more sows get along well. Boars kept together sometimes fight once they reach adulthood. If they get to know one another when they are very young—about six weeks old—they usually can live together happily. It is also important that the animals have plenty of space so they do not crowd one another.

A good breeder or pet shop will be able to give advice on which guinea pigs get along well together. Much depends on the individual animals, because guinea pigs can have big personalities!

A Good Choice

When choosing new pet guinea pigs, examine
them with care to make sure they are fit and
healthy. The animals should be alert and lively,
with a clean, glossy coat and bright eyes. Those
with a runny nose, sticky eyes, or matted fur
should be avoided, because they are likely
to be sick.

It is also important to check whether the
animals are male or female. Guinea pigs breed
very easily, and from an early age. If females
and males are kept together, a couple of guinea
pigs could soon become a crowd!

A healthy guinea pig has glossy fur, bright eyes, and an alert expression.

Guinea pigs need plenty of space to run around in, as well as one or two covered places for hiding and resting.

A New House

Guinea pigs can be kept indoors or outdoors, in a cage or a **hutch**. The ideal location for a guinea pig home is a sheltered spot. It should be protected from the wind and rain, and away from cold drafts and hot temperatures.

Pet shops sell specially designed cages, but homemade ones can be just as good. They can be made from a wooden frame, with mesh for walls and a solid floor. They should be well ventilated and have plenty of space to allow the guinea pigs to move around. A general rule is to allow each guinea pig four times its own body length of space.

Guinea pigs like their privacy. A good cage should have a separate nesting box—or guinea pig bedroom! A nesting box can be made from an upturned cardboard box with one side cut away. The box can easily be replaced if it gets dirty.

Animal Friends

In the wild, guinea pigs are prey animals. That means they are hunted by other animals—on the ground and from the air. As a result, they have a shy, cautious nature. However, with careful handling, they should learn to live with any other pets in a household.

Guinea pigs should always be supervised when other animals are around. Other pets should be introduced gradually, one short visit at a time and at a distance. Eventually with patience, the animals should become less wary of each other. They might even become friends!

By far the best and most natural companion for any pet guinea pig is always another guinea pig. Sometimes guinea pigs and rabbits are kept in the same pen, and they usually accept each other. However, rabbits are bigger, stronger, and more boisterous than shy guinea pigs. Rabbits can jump playfully when they are happy, and their powerful hind legs can accidentally cause serious injury to a guinea pig.

Keeping Clean

Guinea pigs rely on humans to make sure their home is always clean. They can be messy little animals. They often jump into their food bowls and kick bedding and droppings around their cage. Any wet hay and food scraps should be cleared out every day. The cage or hutch should be washed out once a week with soapy water and mild disinfectant.

Guinea pigs groom themselves by licking their fur, and domestic varieties do not generally need to be bathed. Bathing is stressful for them, so it should be avoided if possible.

The exception to this rule is if a pet guinea pig has lice or some other kind of **parasite**. In this case, a vet may recommend bathing the guinea pig using a special mild shampoo. The animal should be stood in a shallow bowl with a little warm water and bathed very gently. No water or soap should touch its face or ears. Afterward, it should be gently patted with a towel and kept warm until it is completely dry.

Many guinea pigs enjoy spending time outdoors on the grass. Keep them in a covered mesh run, and watch them so they do not escape!

Ideal Home

Before a guinea pig is brought home from the pet shop or breeder, everything should be prepared for its arrival.

The floor of the hutch should be covered with plain wood chips or hay to make soft, comfortable bedding and absorb any mess. In the wild, cavies live in burrows, so they like plenty of hay to make a cozy nest to sleep in. Don't use fine, dusty sawdust, cedar wood shavings, or scented chips. These materials can irritate a guinea pig's sensitive skin. Scratchy straw can also cause injury to eyes and ears.

A full food bowl should be placed in the cage. Heavy ceramic bowls are best, since lighter plastic or metal dishes tend to get chewed, or kicked over during playtime!

There should be a water bottle filled with freshwater. Cavies can drink up to 3½ fluid ounces (100 ml) a day, so they need constantly replenished supplies of water.

Many owners use wood chips as bedding. A layer of hay can be added on top, so the guinea pigs can nest in it or even enjoy a quick snack.

Feeding healthy treats by hand can help a guinea pig feel safe and happy with its owner.

Day One

Leaving familiar surroundings for a new home can be frightening for guinea pigs, so the journey should be made as comfortable as possible. Guinea pigs are best transported in a box or carry case lined with plenty of soft hay. The case should have a lot of airholes. A simple plastic storage container with wire over the top is just as good as a special animal box. However, don't use a cardboard box because guinea pigs can chew their way out!

When guinea pigs arrive at a new home, it will take them about two days to feel comfortable. The strange surroundings, smells, and sounds are likely to be stressful for them, and they should be left alone to settle in, with regular food and water. A snack of a carrot stick makes a good welcome gift. After the settling-in period, they will be ready to make friends.

Playtime

Guinea pigs become tamer the more time they spend with people. Because they are timid, they do not like loud noises. But they will respond to regular visits and a soft, quiet voice. Eventually they will love being handled and cuddled, but it is a gradual process and takes patience. After many visits and plenty of stroking they can be picked up with both hands, one hand supporting them under the bottom. They feel safest when they are held close to a person's body.

Guinea pigs need a stimulating environment. They instinctively like to hide, so logs and tunnels make good toys for them. They also love to play in a covered run. A run is a long, narrow playpen with a wire-mesh roof and sides. It can be any size, and placed in the garden or indoors. A guinea pig can happily play in a run for hours!

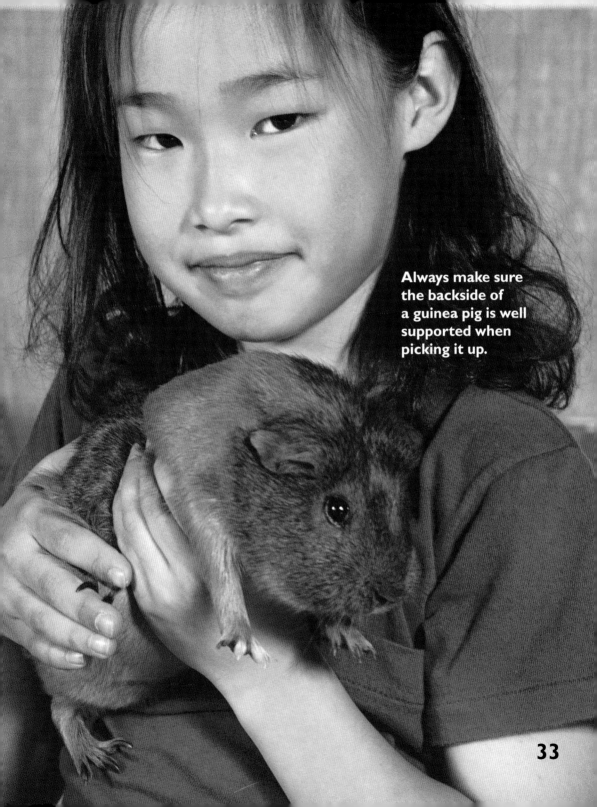

Always make sure the backside of a guinea pig is well supported when picking it up.

Dry foods, such as grains and guinea pig mix, should be placed in a bowl, which will keep them fresh.

Favorite Foods

Like all rodents, cavies are **herbivores**, or plant eaters. Their diet consists of hay, grains, and vegetables. Hay is very important because it provides fiber to help their digestion. Timothy hay is best for guinea pigs. Alternatives such as alfalfa are too rich for them. The animals should be given plenty of hay. The hay should be checked to make sure it is clean and dry, because it often doubles up as bedding and a meal!

Guinea pigs cannot produce vitamin C in their body. To make sure they get this vitamin, guinea pigs should be fed a selection of fresh vegetables and fruit every day. Each guinea pig has different tastes, but carrot, apple, broccoli stalks, and dandelion leaves are all popular. Lettuce should not be fed to guinea pigs. It contains toxins that can be harmful to them.

Special food can be bought from pet stores that contains the right nutrients for guinea pigs' health. Guinea pigs should be fed twice a day.

Sharp Senses

Guinea pigs need well-developed senses to help them recognize friends and avoid enemies. Though they have small ears, they have sharp hearing. They quickly learn to recognize sounds, especially the rustling of a food bag! They have a good sense of smell, which they use to identify one another, as well as humans and other animals.

Their eyes are placed at the sides of their head, so they can see in front and to each side without moving their neck. In the wild, that would allow them to spot danger from all sides. Guinea pigs also have whiskers that help them sense what is around them, especially at night. If the whiskers—which are wider than the width of the guinea pig—can fit through a space untouched, so can the rest of the animal's body.

Guinea pigs also have fast reactions. They are quick runners, so may be hard to catch if they escape. They are good at hiding, so should always be kept in sight! In addition, they startle very easily and can sometimes "freeze" in one position if they are frightened.

Two guinea pigs exchange greetings by touching noses and smelling each other.

A guinea pig enjoying a cuddle may squeak or grunt softly.

Communication

Guinea pigs are vocal animals. That means they use their voices a lot. They make a wide range of noises to communicate and to express their feelings. Some scientists believe they have identified more than 20 different guinea pig noises.

One noise to listen out for is a squealing, whistling sound that some people call **wheeking**. Guinea pigs make this noise when they are excited. A loud purring means they are contented. They often make this noise when they are being petted or fed.

Guinea pigs can also make little jumps in the air when they are excited. This is a typical guinea pig gesture and some people call it **popcorning**.

Staying Healthy

As long as they are kept, clean, warm, and well fed, pet guinea pigs are normally happy and healthy. But it is important to keep a close eye on their health. Regular home checkups can help guinea pigs stay in good condition.

Playtime is the ideal chance for owners to give their guinea pigs a health check. Guinea pigs should always be lively and bright-eyed, with clean, soft fur, straight white teeth, and a good appetite. Problems to watch out for include swollen, sticky eyes or nose, a dirty backside, and sore skin or feet.

The claws will need to be trimmed if they get too long. This job should be done by an adult only. The sharp tips of the claws should be carefully clipped off. Care should be taken not to cut too close to the sensitive **quick**. A vet can help the first time, to make sure the clipping is done properly.

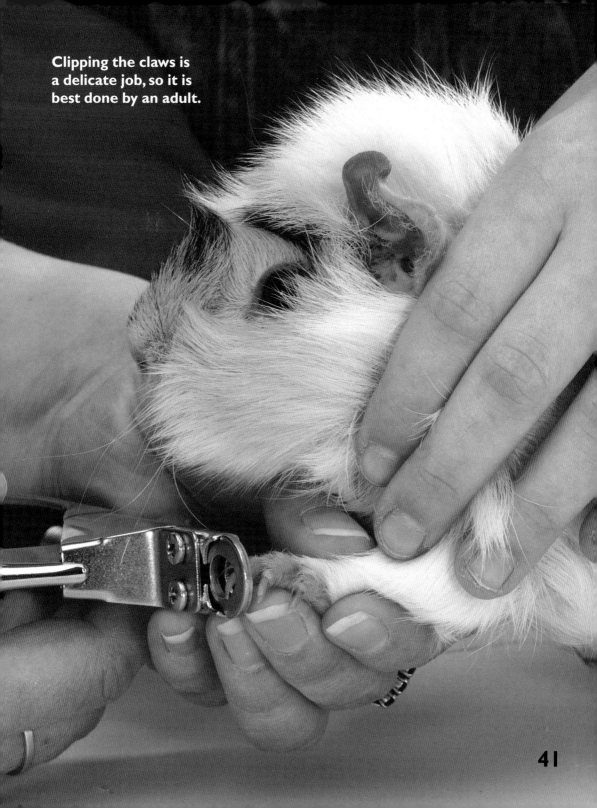

Clipping the claws is a delicate job, so it is best done by an adult.

Pups should be handled only after they have formed a secure bond with their mother—at least five days after being born.

Time to Breed

Some owners decide to breed their guinea pigs, but this is a big decision. Breeding guinea pigs is best left to experts. Serious breeders sell the babies, or produce show guinea pigs for competitions.

Guinea pigs can breed from as young as four weeks old until about five years. If a boar and a sow are put together, they will quickly mate. The pregnant female's body will grow wide and fat, and take on a shape that looks like an eggplant. Pregnancy lasts for about 68 days.

Guinea pig babies are called **pups**. Sows can have several **litters**, or groups of pups, without a break throughout the year if they are breeding. The mother will give birth to a litter of between one and seven pups, with an average of three.

Guinea Pig Pups

Guinea pig births are very quick. Babies usually appear overnight without anyone seeing the event. Newborn pups weigh about 3½ ounces (100 g). They are very well developed, with fur and teeth, and with their eyes open. In fact, they look just like miniature versions of their parents.

The pups can run around and eat solid food within a day, although they usually **nurse**, or feed from their mother, for up to three weeks. Baby males and females should be separated at six weeks old to prevent them from mating.

A mother watches over her litter of small but perfectly formed pups.

A handsome Coronet guinea pig and its dedicated owner are rewarded with a trophy.

Showtime!

There are many guinea pig clubs or pet clubs that hold regular shows. These events give owners or breeders a chance to meet and talk to fellow guinea pig-lovers as well as to compete in the show.

Guinea pig shows usually have classes for different breeds. At shows, the animals are judged against a standard for that variety. The winners might be awarded with a trophy.

Shows also often include a class where pets are judged purely on their overall condition and temperament. Any guinea pig and its owner can join this class!

In the Lab

Cavies were one of the first types of animals to be used in scientific and medical experiments, which is why we often refer to an animal or person used in research as a "guinea pig." A guinea pig's body works a lot like a human body, and guinea pigs can develop many of the illnesses that humans suffer from. These diseases include the lung disorder tuberculosis, or TB, and scurvy, which results from not getting enough vitamin C in the diet. This similarity to humans makes guinea pigs very useful in medical research.

Guinea pigs are still used today to develop and test medicines. Thanks to guinea pigs, over the years, scientists have made many medical breakthroughs that have helped save countless human lives.

Words to Know

Agouti
The original cavy color of gray-brown, with black flecks.

Boars
Male guinea pigs.

Cavies
Another word for guinea pigs.

Digits
Toes on a guinea pig's feet.

Guard hairs
Long, coarse hairs on the surface of the fur, which protect the skin.

Herbivores
Plant-eating animals.

Hutch
A wooden box with a mesh front, used to house guinea pigs.

Incisors
The long teeth at the front of the mouth in rodents.

Litters
Groups of babies born at the same time to one mother.

Nonself
A name for a cavy coat that has two or more colors, such as tortoiseshell (red and black).

Nurse
To drink milk from the mother's body.

Parasite	A tiny creature that lives in or on a cavy's body, often causing discomfort or disease.
Pelts	Guinea pigs' furry coats.
Popcorning	When a happy or excited guinea pig arches its back and repeatedly jumps into the air.
Pups	Baby guinea pigs.
Quick	The part at the center of a guinea pig's claw. This area is sensitive and bleeds easily.
Rosettes	Swirls in the fur of certain breeds of guinea pigs.
Self	A word for a coat of just one color.
Sows	Female guinea pigs.
Undercoat	A layer of soft, fine fur next to a cavy's skin, which keeps it warm.
Wheeking	A unique noise that guinea pigs make when they are excited or calling for attention.

Find Out More

Books

Barnes, J. *Pet Guinea Pigs*. Pet Pals. Strongsville, Ohio: Gareth Stevens Publishing, 2006.

Hibbert, C. *Guinea Pig*. Looking After Your Pet. Mankato, Minnesota: Smart Apple Media, 2004.

Web sites

ASPCA Animaland: Pet Care
www.aspca.org/site/PageServer?pagename=kids_pc_guinea_411
Information about caring for guinea pigs.

Enchanted Learning: Guinea Pig
www.enchantedlearning.com/subjects/mammals/rodent/Guineapigprintout.shtml
Facts about the guinea pig and a diagram to print.

Index